AF219603

ばかげている

【ミクコンセプト】

思考は思考をもたらす

思考は人生のすべてを支配します

際限なく閉じ込められた

Miku Kumiko

ridiculous 1/2

koans

meditations

thoughts

remarks

ridiculous

Bibliografische Information der Deutschen Nationalbibliothek: Die Deutsche Nationalbibliothek verzeichnet diese Publikation in der Deutschen Nationalbibliografie; detaillierte bibliografische Daten sind im Internet über dnb.dnb.de abrufbar.

【ミクコンセプト】

Herstellung und Verlag:

BoD – Books on Demand, Norderstedt

ISBN: 9783753446196

And the day is already wasted

Everything that is - is not true to me - and
has not said - what is not available - we
ask and have one - and we suspect - it is
not in the I - I am gradually in the is - the
day is tired and I am not there - and my
mind is no longer here - it's just wasted in
my brain - and everything is done so well -
it's exactly as you think - and the day is
wasted again.

The end is already near

Amazed, wounded by the worries - it
played away at the beginning - or it didn't
start after all - believed in your heart - the
end result was correct - and yet the days
looked playful - slowly half dead - find
nothing behind it - and still high laugh on
your neck - be happy and sure of what
you have - the end is already near.

Or do you have me and are you popular

Funny seen you - love is already hot and overcooked - and the heart is well cared for - I miss and I miss you - it's good that you have me - and you perceive me as pain - what kind of current is that - gladly seen and felt good - come to something and then you have me - am full of urges - seek pain for a whole life - give up and hurt me - or is it the big urge - or you have me and are popular.

Find and try

The days have passed and I haven't always been happy. I was familiar with requests from people around me for years, hoping to take them in and still think about them. People with hearts and well-meaning joys did me good, and it was the whole new story to think about, or even more, to think about. Always a new story, the old stories, new experiences and results did not exist or if so, only in my head. Drinking and eating remains, is good and has and quickly brings calm. Seen in this way and believed in new stories, believed again and again. The thought that bit me has sharp teeth, the wound in the brain is not bleeding. We want to make more beautiful stories. Nightmares don't need support. And the days have passed and a new day is here again. Time has me and that's a good thing. I'm caught up in the lies of the stories and I keep sitting and maybe that's how I love it. Are you me or am I just me in this story? I don't want to make it easy for myself, tomorrow it will be different today and the question arises what is left. It doesn't matter because everything is always new and the small parts of the present that are perceived shine differently than others, especially the good ones. Happy, this is a thousand fold beginning for all stories. Find and try.

Look into the near future when you grew up

My posture became more and more relaxed, my shoulders slumped and I could admire the other life, the other sun and the good TV commercials. The bald head reflected the whole world again and the nose turned against the wind. On which day did I not buy particularly beautiful glasses to keep my posture? The sun outshines my other life and I'm in love with an ad. Look into the near future when you grew up.

Go home and be the night

Look famous - crawl into your hand with
praise - the future is different - we won
and still have nothing - then it was night -
the famous look has become different -
the night is not always different - want
and have - the writing got smaller - and
there is so much to read - well done and
lost in hand - everything is nonsense - try
not to understand anything - go home and
be the night.

Sure well done

The daring goes the short ways - look into
the hearts of the available ones - want to
use you and me and kidnap - the good
guys were serious - and everyone thought
- be superior - maybe they meant - or in
the worst case inferior - the good noses of
the daredevils - show more than moving
hours - sacrifice more than good - I just
did everything well - and were definitely
used - remain available - demand will grow
and revive us - were certainly well
outdone.

Disappear

Good brave little monkeys lie down after
tomorrow hoping for a better day and
focus your attention on the essentials. We
believe and reckon with indescribable
discomfort the day after tomorrow and
paint a picture of the unrest we like or
even hope to love, and even just one hope
to love and fight like an animal, and we
and the monkeys pluck and clap and live
and they don't want to go anymore.

That makes sense

Well-heeled and yet beside herself, the princess used fate as an excuse. Inspired by beautiful ideals, the next sense has been identified and properly polished, you have to shine and that's a purpose. The first young thoughts have turned into a strong tree that is already bearing fruit. Maybe it's nonsense that keeps you alive, that gives you the flavour and helps us survive. Well-heeled, the princess and your fate, everything shines and produces fat when fertilized. The earth is drowning and artificial abstinence is becoming an integral part of this idealized world. That makes sense.

And sometimes get lost

Feel your fingers and go there - hit sharp
corners - look for the dust on the floor -
play with the everyday dirt - build a new
day - finger the other person - shove deep
holes - and lose sometimes.

Give me a kiss

The ravages of time gnaw at my
consciousness, I hope for a subconscious
and look to a favourable moment, I will
want to know what is in store for us and
of course that will only mean something
to me. The hunger towel tastes very much
like a used towel of a mass unit, the tooth
is full of holes and the exaggerated
thoughts of the theatre have no future.
The donors were always nice to me until
they stopped giving. Why had I wondered
why for years? Was it a rediscovery of
another level of consciousness? The
ravages of time still gnaw and the root is
broken. The trust in new madness ceases,
the old has nothing and the new tastes
boring and stale, explains it again and
again and makes your stomach hang and
wants to be a part of it. Hit the pain and
you will be there, a good joke, nothing to
laugh about, but still a joke of the
hopeless. In the evening I had a quick
glass of schnapps so I could see the
hunger cloth clearly, and the good guys
were there too, giving explanations on the

most important points of their worldview. I got as bad as death. Being human is not fun without stories. And the old people talked and gestured and brought up the past again. So passed the hours, the days and the years and all of life. Nothing was really attacked, why should I? Give me a kiss.

I hear you

You have fun at the meeting - you are a
good storyteller - you have a big head -
there is a lot and emptiness in it - the
eyelids droop - the eyes are almost asleep -
good crushers come in - the appearance
makes you tired - leads to new
conversations - the voice is hoarse - my
ear is closed - what is the conversation for
- and - do you hear me - or - do I hear
you?

Remains

The short sentence of essentials has been
abbreviated to death, it's done, hands
joined, the laughter hangs and the sad
ones are right, what is it again, do you
have me or what is or are we rejecting it?
The mourning gets shorter, the sentence is
finished and the clever ones make a nice
rhyme of it, the day has a note, the night
time fear remains.

Are

Everything gets dirty, then we do
something you don't want and we are
really happy and we show ourselves and
we don't know who we are anymore.

You cannot change it

How is the goat? How is the child? How
is the big man? Breathe yourself and you
breathe me. A courageous woman does
not forgive - the great man sees nothing -
and the skills become finer - how are you -
and slowly it becomes quiet - the night
comes - the colours become greyer - that's
how it is.

And the church bells ring

Good Sunday, bring me a roast hare and talk to me. We laugh at other people on the street and don't really notice each other. Attention is the magic word and love is next, love for the pros and maybe the cons. Always let it be mean and unsuccessful. The selfless is too difficult, difficult and difficult or something else. A good roast rabbit on Sunday, bread dumplings taste good with it, children are happy and boldly eat their way through to dessert. What is difficult and what is sentimental, what is brief and what is brave? And the church bells ring.

And sometimes well attended

I am in unusual days - the new is always
dear to me - the old is always new - in
search of the state of the fire - and the
fingers become stiffer - the hips ache - the
lungs only half breathe - and there is no
more victory - or it never existed - or
there cannot be anything like that - what
do beautiful spirits actually imagine -
nightmares are also justified - everyone
has them - sometimes just sore -
sometimes dirty - and sometimes well
attended.

And yet you lose yourself

If a more vulgar text is more peppery or
you tend to withdraw, let yourself be
touched or feared that you will enjoy it.
What about the ordinary itself that it likes
openly and is satisfied with, is it an end in
itself or a real satisfaction and is it you?
How dirty can you be that you still want
yourself, what are your limits in your
imagination and how tired is your
aggressiveness? Constricted by custom
and tortured by society, how are you
trapped in your head, how are you without
restriction. The respect is high and
remains good. If wars come your way
again, show yourself and tell us. And yet
you lose yourself.

And you are dead

It was hidden - sweat persists - noses suck
it in - the day is sharp - life is in love - take
good precautions - form a strong opinion
- the sweat smells strong - smart thoughts
do not arise - opinions die - the sweat is
old - and you are dead.

Too deep

Especially today I heard voices from heaven again, they wanted to tell me something, I don't know what, it definitely didn't sound very friendly. My concentration has decreased in the past few years, too many sentences challenged my brain cells and apparently some of them got killed too, or was it the bad air from the street or was I aging? Be warm and at least hope that you will be loved in order to finally manage to ignore the curses and strangers or not. All are people, sick, molesters, angels, saviours and thoughts. Usually to get used to it and look deep into the glass. Too deep.

Sense

Another sentence without meaning and
short and tangy and fill out the paper and
listen to yourself or there are sentences
without meaning again.

All holiness disappears in prayer

Beautiful thoughts nourish the hero -
crying children express hearts - where is
the happy superficiality - and why do you
add your little joy - heroes are celebrated
and then recommended - the house
blessing is now back - thoughts become
easier and free - create happiness for
yourself - children cry sad and lonely - all
holiness disappears in prayer.

To let

Today don't run away and close your ears
and discuss and listen to music, get the
day right and let go of the absurd, clean
your fingernails and let your smelly toes
stink.

Rapture and slip

The greeting slipped into my face, the ulterior motives of a better position simply seized, they had not concentrated so much for a long time and yet nothing happened. The greeting subsided, seemed a little more relaxed and without surrendering, the ulterior motives were perhaps easy to guess. But everyone was in their thoughts and nothing happened. Convincing, clever artists told of wealth and satisfaction, the audience loosened their shoulders and believed in it for a moment. The past quickly caught up with everyone. Rapture and slip.

The farewell is particularly comforting

In the beginning there was the pain that
bored into my head and was funny too.
Who could blame me for not being
talkative and also thinking about
nonsense? The worst part was listening,
listening, nodding, and pretending to
understand. Do good for the other
person, make them believe you have made
a friend, make them feel in good hands,
and go crazy yourself. A constant lie, there
is no end to being trapped in yourself. The
farewell is particularly comforting.

Everything makes sense

The conversation about the topic of the
day - announce and stay curious - air
yourself without premonition - and the
heart is as big as an athlete - write down -
everything makes sense.

And we keep looking

Our future swims towards us - only strong
winners meet us - we look almost
fanatically for losers - we need support - a
good grip in passing - what became of
admiration - when we stand behind people
- and when we are in front - is the
lifeblood no longer red - it's crystal clear
and very thin - people mourn old friends -
and we keep looking.

Future

When it comes to defiance we all agree
and find the overlap and join forces and
see a future worth living in.

And go when you want

Forced happiness - isn't bad after all - has
something - feels good - does not run in -
and does not get worse - is something -
and goes whenever you want.

The beginning was made again

Sitting for the first time - all alone -
everyone is amazed and cheered - the
heart is big - the joke is lost - tears find
their way - the art is nothing - the
beginning has been made again.

By doing

I want and want and am and have and
admit that there is nothing other than an I
and multiply and understand myself or at
least not and otherwise there is nothing
and I hear nothing, I and I and am I and I
am.

The nest is empty

In the north lies the cold, in the south the sun burns the day, there is a ring for the hand and soon the good man has nothing more to say. And why? He likes to do it so much and can enjoy his life in peace, drink the joy and put everything off. It is lucky that there are angels who help you be weak, who help you to withdraw quickly. Mothers help, fathers suffocate, children scream and the water splashes, always a relationship we like, always a day like any other. Thank God and find the meaning or have enough of all this meaning, the daring, the sayings, the aphorisms, the sacred teachings. The nest is empty.

The singing sounds high

I'm in the broom cupboard - looking for a
beginning - the room is dark - adventure is
over - the broom cupboard is not small -
there are enough obstacles - satisfaction is
not lost either - the beginning is good -
the room remains dark - the adventure
becomes more intense - dialogues become
arguments - are you alone - am I alone -
the broom cupboard stays at home - the
singing sounds high.

Be deactivated

The obstacles keep getting bigger, the farmers raise cattle for daily use and the beneficiaries complain about stories from the gossip columns. The spring sun is already strong, warming the cold spots in the city, if only briefly, and the evening is falling quickly. Quick questions come from very smart people and don't need an answer. The farmers are good enough because the suppliers and service recipients cackle endlessly. Accusation is a great way to upset the sensitive, crush the sentimental, and weaken the strong. To be deaf is easy, you can't hear anything. Be deactivated.

How well can you wait

First a horror - then a treasure - more a
strong self-centred one - then a more
understanding one - and your pants are
full, death is near and love is lost - what is
it - and where - how well can you wait?

Days and evenings die off

Did you do well? Then you must have become happy. Breathing in made us pause. Heavy fumes fog our brains. Loss takes care of me. Extraordinary days hit me. The crisis is nice. I'm drunk. Everyone understands the past. The future - days and evenings perish.

Entangled

The normal consumer is back, he is well
served, he sticks his nose into every hole
and like everyone else is very fair and
trusts me and serves me and protects
himself, normal and needed and involved.

What is it then

Boastful and well done, the earthly feel the
outside and get stuck in the morass. Fall
will definitely come again before it gets
dark and we can think until we pass out
and start a new day for ourselves. A day
full of old fears, there should also be
hopes, there are beautiful inspirations and
a pink icing. What is the trump card, who
has the decisive cards, what does victory
mean? What is it then?

There is no mercy

Be that as it may, the anger makes the boys scream and yet they know nothing. Fear grows and rescue does not come, everyone drifts apart lost. Sunsets are part of it, passions are always reborn, beautiful or ugly, one way or another. A romantic song is intoned in the head. There is no mercy.

Or at least further

Basically the mind is lost - find the mind
again thoroughly - the others are
superficially telling something - be in good
shape - revaluate the day - the mind is lost
- who has found something again - the
door closes - or it opens.

And abdicate at some point

Having fun again and not getting away
from it - having to party and eat - what a
wonderful life - well booked hours full of
fun - work and think up one pleasure after
another - waiting for friends and being
almost lonely - your head is filled with
familiar thoughts - the beginning always
comes new - nothing gets old - I've eaten
everything and I feel bad - and I can't stop
having fun - spending hours buying
pleasure - making friends again - work
makes a lot of sense - self - trust is
cultivated - something could be finite and
everything will be better tomorrow - give
yourself a lot of help with your thoughts -
eating is great fun - and finally abdicate.

A fertile mind

The fertile soil is being prepared, the seeds
of tomorrow's harvest will be worked
deep into the earth. And then wait, wait
what comes tomorrow, whether pests
have come, whether the fruits are ingested
by thieves before harvest or whether
everything is just a game. A game about
looking and having fun. And the image is
becoming more and more blurred,
spongy, faded or has dissolved and there
is residue, nobody wants it. The rooms are
getting bigger and the people in them
more voluminous, the soil more sterile
and the crops richer. Pests got the coup
de grace, what a grace. The madness in the
head looks like jewelry, the thieves no
longer laugh, not even because they
hunted, not even hunted in eternity. Well-
dressed human hosts take home intelligent
tools to believe that business will flourish
because everyone needs a talisman,
something pictorial, a spell, a magic.
Everything works fine again, the games
broaden your horizons and, strangely

enough, the trouble is gone. A fertile
world of the spirit.

Out

Especially in the back, where nobody can
look, a little wimp is hiding and enjoying
his life, is not irritated by the stench, has
found happiness, in the back, in the back
of the buttocks and counts your thoughts
and your life and your lost life.

Find

Do not say anything in a few words and
unwind the thread and find solace in
words again.

Or are you already perfect

The night has come, the street lamps
shine to infinity, we sit quietly and
satisfied in front of the television and
thank God for the stressful day. Everyone
thinks of their own future happiness or,
hopefully, a few happy hours. A few dark
figures fight their way through the
darkness and appear black, the darkness
drives the forgotten out of the loopholes,
they are also looking for happiness or are
it our fantasies that are drifting dark in the
dark. There is a lucky charm in your hand,
when the day is over it will serve. Or are
you already perfect?

Because the rest is attached there

At the very back is a haunted house -
when does the full moon come again -
when does the moon shine on the house -
when does the glow become more
bearable again - and at the very back of
the haunted house - there are the drunken
screams of today - don't play games - you
don't need a game more - swim and
drown - and calm returns to the haunted
house - the ghost can go to sleep -
because calm is appropriate there.

Die hard

You let it go - it crushes you - you are so
free. Is it you - and you see me - and you
do not change - we hug - and mean
nothing - you think well alone - and you
give yourself the consolation - opinions
are good - opinions are good - don't hide
everything - slowly go under.

The stomach growls

It burned fingernails for a long time and
the personality grinned, young servants
made it easy and hard-earned authority
has a red face. Wounds are not only there
to be licked, they also look beautiful,
sometimes never heal and yet do not
survive. Artists tie thick scarves around
their necks and look thoughtfully into the
air, they fart quietly and not only ignore
each other. And the night comes and
catches you, everyone is home. The
stomach growls.

And a new beginning

The special moment has come - those
hungry for life shake hands - there was
nothing else - except sausage and bacon -
a day like any other - many believed they
were royal - the complaints never stopped
- many went crazy - questions arose - and
nobody was tied up - you were sent to the
border in the unknown - interrupted and
vomited - what remains is an empty
stomach - and a new beginning.

And respect increases

Understanding was rolled out and half of the book was read in the pocket, the environment slowly passed and the noises became quieter. What was bearable and how? A fellow traveller asked a half-sleeping dreamer. He grunted slightly, looked between his heavy eyelids, and didn't answer. If you understand for tomorrow and for a small group, you do not need more and everything is already explained. Sentences rattle one after the other into the ravine and don't need anything. The travellers sing a wandering song and look for the feeling of unity, the feeling of togetherness and the successful thoughts that convey the feeling of security. A few more are flooded and not listening, part of it, a break, a meal found. And respect increases.

And hopefully it won't turn blue

My heart that shines - polished and good -
shines deep red and pumps and pumps - I
swallow well - and seldom breathe - laugh
at strangers for no reason - whether that's
good - I don't know - I've lost my heart in
my chest - it opens and closes - my
feelings suffocate me every now and then
- but the sun is shining again - part of the
air is clean - another part is dirty -
everything is well mixed - swallow well
and seldom breathe - the heart stays red -
and hopefully it doesn't turn blue.

A special sentence

Again a brief thought comes to mind and
I cough softly to myself, it can't really be a
deep and long outpouring, the spirits don't
bother me today because my heart stays
red and I rarely breathe. A special
sentence.

Or even in old age

There are friends who have fun - then
there are hats with brims - friends protect
themselves and are happy - people quickly
take to the streets - and chase their dream
friends - find each other on islands and
say hello loudly - and stay and keep your
thoughts firmly - without intention -
everything just happened - and the friends
were lost again - no meaningful thought
remained with them - the hats have brims
- and they have no brims either - friends
sometimes have a beard - and often no
beard - some friends have beards and
others rarely wear hats - and the streets
are getting wider - the traffic is getting
faster - we are waiting for an island - with
or without greetings - and the evening will
come again - or even in old age.

Buttoned

Unfortunately, my fingers cannot find the
light switch and I feel and still find a soft
piece of meat with buttons and take a
deep breath and hear the deep red heart
throb and somehow see it blue. I reach for
a misunderstood poem and find the soft
piece of meat again, rather buttoned up.

Alone now

There was such a faint noise to be heard, the pensioner was sitting on the bench in the sun and nodded in agreement, a beginning should come again soon. The birds chirped incredibly quietly, it sounded like a silencer, the light was reflected incredibly brightly on all sunny surfaces and corners. You should have been good, then you would have nothing to fear either, said the old people unanimously, their injuries were forgotten, they felt good and nodded without end. It got really bad for everyone else, some ate, some just looked into space. Soon no one could hear the birds chirping, the low pitch continued to rise and the old people nodded incessantly. The picture was almost terrifying. The hands were in his pants; the hands were sweating nervously. And the old people nodded because they knew everything. And then the rain came, the old people went in, dipped their croissants in the coffee, and continued nodding. Alone now.

And I haven't thought through anything for the day either

Philanthropist, please take my hand - squeeze your hand in a friendly and humane way - show me the way to salvation - hammer the good sentences into my head - I see my hopes for the future - philanthropist take my head - let go put our heads together - something will come out - let's sacrifice our will and swim away - drink milk with honey and swear by nothing - nothing is good enough and the best foundation - philanthropist, this is a feast of thoughts - banish nightmares and circumcise me - and then I woke up - I didn't laugh - and I couldn't think of anything for the day either.

And watch out

Fear haunts the smart and the rich - let
yourself be caught and join forces - there
is a nice festival - you and fear and day
and night - what comes - who stays - are
we a family - or is that the fear of a
stranger without a home - I take you with
me - and allow me to look - and to
observe myself.

The day ends

A beautiful moon - it shines delicately
through the cloudy brain salad - shines
and we shine with you - the night is dark -
and looking is not easy - families listen
together - the moment comes again - the
day is over.

Night

Warm up, get hot and defy all chances,
increase your fighting spirit but it doesn't
work like that, fight like an animal and
everything becomes a sad game because
looking is not easy, especially not at night.

Thank you and amen

The sun is there - the cold is lost - the
grass is sprouting - the wind is whistling
through the bushes - there is the sun - the
grass is growing - people whistle in
passing - hungry for the sun, they keep
their faces in the air - a beautiful one day -
the rays bore their way into the train of
thought - the wind cools the skin - thank
you and amen.

But that's good

My white shirt hangs over the back of the
chair, doesn't look good, doesn't look
good anymore. My legs are dangling hairy
from the windowsill, so they may not look
good or good. The sky is blue, a few
clouds are passing through, it looks pretty
good. My stomach hangs up to the
windowsill, lies there and I feel full. But
that's good.

Maybe eat too

The worst is - I don't know - I'm looking
for it - and will find it - the worst ever -
the biggest mess - will ask you - and
maybe ask - touch it briefly - and then eat
- maybe also food.

All the conversations in your head are free

The depressive movement in the corner -
the heart is clean - the lungs empty - what
is screaming back there in the corner - not
a bit forgotten - don't try to start - go
home quickly and let yourself be caressed
- life is not always easy - the more you
want - the easier it is for you - and you will
no longer get along - all the conversations
in your head are in vain.

Or not

Everything is good and nothing comes true - the grass that grows - the role of the victim takes its place - and the ham roll tastes very good - the past has been rolled up - well lit and without shadows - the words are collected - the flashes of inspiration stay given up - hug me - and understand me - everything will be fine - or the end will come in big strides - the victim role is not a ham role - and the past gives you a kick - hug yourself - you can do it or not.

Nothing about it

Playful and well received, I've learned
background information and can't really
do anything with it. The sausages are too
phlegmatic to approach the day. They
have been cooked well and are slowly
starting to cool. What's that got, why don't
you go with me, what's that word in your
throat, a good beginning and a difficult
ending. Or not, we know. And my legs
carry me into the jungle of thoughts,
breathing heavily in the thick air, a
moment of happiness arises because I was
there once and can tell about it. Nobody
listens, the day remains tired and the
shadows begin to grow. It's not supposed
to sound dark or anything. The hours
counted get their own smell, the bacteria
do a great job. Go with me and don't get
lonely, wash my remaining hours and taste
my thoughts, what nonsense. But live the
unity, without ifs and buts, without buts
and delusions, without you and me.
Nothing about it.

Summer is already here

Children sing a song - spring is coming
soon - or is it already there - the beginning
tastes sweet - the newborns are waiting -
the little finger shows nothing - well
advised and guessing - day and night and
the future - children sing a song - spring is
slowly getting old - the beginning has been
made - the beginning tastes sweet -
summer is already here.

Are easy to digest

What does the great infinity mean for the little man and he can get away with it without knowing anything about it, it doesn't matter, the driven ones need him and nursery rhymes sound good. Are easy to digest.

An eternal repetition

Quick money can be earned quickly - the fasting day will pass quickly - the fast is already over - the ancients have already said that this brings us nothing new - the high mountain doesn't just look high - the little things are often overlooked - the quick money trickles through your fingers - the moments also pass pretty quickly - what remains is a strange feeling - the open questions shrink - nothing cannot be solved - nothing cannot be solved - an eternal repetition.

Or everything will be fine

Sunbeams turn my thoughts on, bright moments briefly shake my hand and tear off the nets, trees and bushes bloom and with them a whole colony of ants. There is now enough to eat, to eat, to build up fat reserves on the unused fat that is there. We believe that there is a good way out for everything somewhere, holy waiting, your angel is protecting you. Countless angels are buzzing around you and where are the devils hiding, who wants to give birth more? Hopefully it's not you and what about the angels and so on. The suns shine in your head and warm your skin, some even get hope and some get worried pretty quickly. The bright moments reward you. Then come the big festivals and a certain gratitude, fat and death. Or everything will be fine.

And run in circles

We did it well - so well that nobody can
talk about it - we shake hands - and shake
it - and believe in tomorrow again - we
contributed well - so well that nobody
likes us anymore - the opponents raise
their index fingers - and demonize our
mornings - we watch - and run in circles.

The backpack only gets heavier

The ball is rolling towards us, the game has become serious business, and casual wear has become a uniform. We dream, we have to dream, no matter what happens, want it and taste it, the ball that rolls, apparently somehow and against it. The blossoms of the tree deceive us, the fearful rabbit was able to save himself and the brave one died of a low shot. And run and run and run and right into the goal, it wasn't a ball, it was the friendly day. The backpack only gets heavier.

Good sentences are not lost

A colourful bird fluttered in the evening play - a sweet piece for all of us - a cosy home has been found - and there should be no compromises - you have to be found first - and then it must not be - an evening piece and a morning piece - the night piece and that daily piece - art tastes good - good sentences are not lost.

Delivered new

All the best - good start - affected parents
- broken fingernails - black teeth -
trapped, trapped listless - laughed with
pleasure - all good - loved in the beginning
- broken teeth - black fingernails - good
words - no end - no beginning - new
delivery.

And nothing else

The Buddha for the poor - the prayer for
the rich - let's put it down - let's move an
illusion - sparkling stones - heavy gold
nuggets - we are balanced - and have
nothing else.

The paper ran out

In principle, it doesn't matter, we run into anomalies and dare not enter into a more serious relationship, it doesn't matter and who wants to hear a true word? Those who say yes are long-term speakers who don't care are closer to you. But in principle and usually it doesn't matter. The word for that day has been said hundreds of times and has been useless to this day. The newspaper is in your armpit and the day is not fresh either, the principles are going bad, and you can save yourself further sayings. That ends well, all bad. Now it's enough, the ideas are wrong and just copied, armpits get stuck and will not be seen at other times in the future either. A thought of the meaning. The paper ran out.

And the rule was broken again

Since the heart has not yet been fried - the
hungry thought of yesterday - a thought
came from the heart - and I became
hungry - wanted to devour something
fried - and feast - with heart and thoughts
- hunger and roast - a new happiness - and
the best greetings - the day is easy - the
hormones are somehow balanced -
everything turned out to be good - hearts
remain hungry - no real experience during
the day - but good and a yes - take care of
yourself - and that was the rule that
existed always there.

Laughed briefly

At least one laugh - no buts - good efforts
- golden rule - a wink - a fence post - no
ifs - and over - and down - nothing else -
no buts - the weight - short thought -
small person - also the end - a short laugh.

And you have the sleep

Without sleep I can't laugh or hit
anything, without sleep I'm completely
lost and I don't even take off, especially
the big things can't be seen and there is no
longing anyway. This is life without sleep.
And I look for him and have found him
sometimes, nice and hugging, comfortable
and safe, a good life, a life with sleep.
Faces relax and friendliness is resumed,
fatigue becomes a good friend. And you
have the sleep.

Anyway and done

The sound scratches the nerves - the
nerves scratched with the poisoning -
yesterday was today again - to be left
behind - there is no room for openness -
sleep is over - you are no longer looking
for an argument - smart thoughts pass
again - and some special thoughts have set
me free - I've looked for a long time - and
never found - joy has friends - and the
nerves are bare - it doesn't matter and I'm
done.

And yet it's good again

The greeting has arrived, the little king sits
nodding on the throne near the floor and
grins and feels good, the hint has
penetrated and the speeches are not good
for us. A good choice of words makes no
sense, the urgent feeling of being needed
drives everyone crazy. Finally wanting to
find a goal, but the talking remains, you
are bad, I am bad, everything is bad. And
yet it's good again.

Numbers

After saying a short sentence again
without asking or paying you.

An insatiable worm fights its way through

Celebrated naked bodies - torment their
masses during the day - do not know what
to do - doing good cannot mean anything
- always choose good words - the
speeches get louder - the kings smaller -
an insatiable worm fights its way through.

There is enough to look forward to

After and then immediately - a heavy
dream and a heavy head - deeply asleep -
clouds move - everyone can be happy -
but seriousness determines the day - join
in and then let go - the ball was passed on
undeservedly - the ball was not caught -
the other rests - this is the beginning -
black is the dream - the night is deep -
trust everyone - or do not trust everyone -
serious people were laughed at - bit by bit,
then immediately - there is enough to look
ahead.

At least for a few days

It all depends on the right mix, said the middle-class daily thinker, and represents me with his opinion, a good opinion. The right mix of wine and water counts, the right mix of thoughts counts and the delighted people have talked about it. Not getting well again, not in this time, not in this life, talk, that stays and mix your thoughts properly. Change your mind, see everything as a game and say goodbye to seriousness for a short time. Dreams will come back and go away. On your rock, ask unreal questions and get depressed. The game makes everything a little easier. For a few days at least.

Sing a song

Quickly seen - and shut your throat -
yesterday, stop opening up - find a good
life again - quickly write down lies - we
will invent a good day - it is sung well -
the pleasure is far from over - a party
celebrate - wait a long time - don't know
what - and we get older - sing a song.

I liked it

Where did it go, who stole it from us,
where did it go and how can we restore it?
Is that possible? Or is it not possible?
Singing a song alone is not enough. And
so it came about that nothing was done
because it is easy to forget. I liked it.

Get lost in feelings

Heroes laugh out loud and know more -
the feeling counts - the favour lasted an
hour - the news is taking shape - what has
this got to do with you - where are you
going - we admire the beauty - we get lost
in feelings.

Captured

The healthy is contagious, the beautiful
feeling is more than painful for us, but the
calm has also caught us.

And nodded

There I sat and heard strange voices - I
didn't understand a word and still nodded
eagerly - started to laugh at the right time -
and nodded with a spasm in the neck - it
was my own fault - I thought to myself - I
did not - know not an option - and
nodded.

A real nod

But when I fell asleep while nodding - and
almost fell from the armchair - I felt an
automatic twitching of the neck muscles -
politeness must - also nod off - be a real
nod.

Dependent

To be trapped in the environment,
conjure up important things, despise
funny people, the environment is alive and
we are dependent.

The pleasure disappears

The day is getting brighter - security
loopholes - everyone is looking for the
centre - having a good time - your eyes are
stinging - the pleasure disappears.

Some things are good

I often waited a long time, nothing
appeared, I kept falling into the night and
love became boredom. Waited a while,
nothing came and night turned into day.
Tomorrow a new day will come, the old
one has taken possession of me too, and
yet the unrest will not go away. Some
things are good.

Have swallowed well

Forbidden time - suppressed boredom -
slipping in good hours - not enjoying -
where were we - the shoe no longer
pinches - the pockets are emptier - the joy
shown passes - have swallowed well.

And fall asleep

One sip too much - a touch of too little
feeling - forget the inside - blur the
outside - one sip too much - take regular
responsibility - and fall asleep.

Wind up the daydreams and then go out

It stung somewhere in the back and I couldn't see anything, my nose is blocked and my thinking is blocked, the public has cornered me and now wants the normal. When does the right story hit the mark, suddenly wake up and tell endlessly long diffusions. Wake up believing that I woke up. Count the sheep and glide carefree into the night again. Be crazy and wander, your heart is beating wildly, wants to get out and burst. The belief that you have met others has just vanished. Wind up the daydreams and then go out.

Extinguished

It's gotten harder - shaking hands - wiping someone else's head - piercing other heads - just to be nice - erasing the past - or something else - it's getting harder - ears going numb - feelings flawless - and still feeling good - laugh from the heart - and - erased.

Really

The mouth doesn't smell normal, you
chewed on an old dead mouth and didn't
swallow well, the palpitations come back
at night, and the taste in the mouth
doesn't really go away.

Going out

Exciting adventures await the crazy and the uninhibited, adventures well coloured in poisonous paint. An old man laughs loudly and unrestrainedly in the apartment, the laughter turns into a scream, then a grunt, and finally there is silence over the courtyard. Superiors run around wildly, exciting adventures are forgotten and inhibitions spread. It was a beautiful day, the tulips even smelled of something and the bumblebees were gathering. Home becomes home, the screaming comes back regularly, the silence is already sacred. And the problems of life stories will go away anyway when everyone forgets in death. At home you take in all the homeless and protect them during their last steps or their last drive or their last night.

Now the now is no longer good

Hard noises pass - a bird chirps in the
middle of the head - the adventures are
still ahead - people write history - the
wishes of the remaining are great -
perhaps a thought - the wish dies with -
everything is good and the donkey
screams - honour remains related - finally
the now counts - now the now is no
longer good.

It often comes to a quick end

The little worm crawls into the house, uses his plane everywhere and catches the most beautiful pieces that have been saved forever. The sheer horror is reflected in the eyes of the prisoners, one day it couldn't be more calming, everything gone, nothing left. The cold night made the meadow wet, worm tracks are easy to find and the beautiful dry slime speaks a flowery language. All good things have been eaten or destroyed, the owners cry in dark corners and no longer understand their world. They have been rescued, cleared away, and hoarded, and well cared for more than an eternity. It often comes to a quick end.

And comes to an end

Flowers bloom in the garden - it shines brightly during the day - birds chirp and eat fat worms with relish - celebrate parties and never get too much - the sun shines in the hearts - there is always a lot to laugh about at children - nothing can be heard in the distance - old people fight their way through the meadow with their sticks - roast and steam their heads with wine - that's something - that's good - flowers bloom in the meadow - children laugh, friendly old people - worms are eaten - the day is good - and comes to an end.

The beginning has been made

Flight lessons don't take up space - anger
breaks out unrestrained and calms down -
thank God there are whispers everywhere
- the crying becomes quieter and the
flowers sprout - the morning is red and in
the evening you are drunk - beautiful
thoughts come and stay - the beginning is
done.

The heart calms down

Do not give up - just step in - harden the ego - anoint your fingers - good morning - a cosy evening - wishes are forgotten - the heart calms down.

Or lose

Never happened - nothing happened -
have a good eye and be afraid - foundlings
laugh out loud - the beginning is difficult -
there are many things in the game - there
is no certainty - and you win - or lose.

Certainly

After having many conversations and thinking about nothing and that you are getting closer, think again about it and quickly forget about it. The thoughts fly away and can hardly be grasped again. Every day is meant to be a good day in the future, and the dream, hope and desires remain stubborn in you. So many things are funny, laughter and the beginning, the end comes too. In any case.

Open and closed

Round and yet, carefully considered,
ghosts wrestle with each other, the day
feels so simple. Brighten up a little with a
smile, grow, grow together, grow together.
Open and closed.

You are something

We will be there quickly, the answers will
be found quickly and we will give the fears
a new name, the best will probably be love
or the meaning of life or the meaning of
philosophy. Or. Advantages are easy to
use and I certainly don't stand by them.
It's such a thing, too many have a say
again. Everyone has a very strong opinion
because you are something and hopefully
always will be something, compassion
only exists in the head and the smart ones
at least think about it. They are something
and that is enough to have a clear and
precise opinion. Being relaxed is not
important, being relaxed has no place in
the self, you have to fight and then you
become a respectable personality. Oh yes,
only for who. The big personality with a
brain and a résumé. It is also difficult to
get up and enjoy the solarium with your
thoughts. Be quick and happy, be good
enough, and get highlighted. You are
something.

Maybe from the good hours

The excitement has an end - the beginning
is forgotten - the smart ones still talk
about it - and the good has an appearance
- go there and tell a little - maybe about
the good hours.

Take everything with you and unite

Thought about but still pretty good - wake up and stare at the sky - the sky is so blue and bright - wake up and carve out your first thoughts - nature is loud and penetrates deep into the soul - will be for the first time again being penetrated and laughing - the look is taking shape and I love it - take it all with you and unite.

It remains a hit

It's a hit and I like to be a part of it, the sentence sounds good and I write it down, hear and notice it very often. The hit is good and I'm about to hammer sentences into their heads and bewitch them. Tonight we run out of air and we breathe heavily again, investigating all the details and finding no solution. The air has run out or is too thick. Lie down, bathe in the hit, memorize all the sentences, keep them ready to fire, the right day will come. And if not, then not. It remains a hit.

And the morning comes again

Evening mood and aggression combine - the answers are close - the last day will certainly come again - or not - it has a meaning - or a core - use the evening mood well - the aggression subsides - and it will be tomorrow. Come back.

Heavy

Have worked well and feel that the key
forces are weakening, the eternal struggle
with the earth and the stones, nothing
really stands in the way, the stones are
heavy.

Then the day would be perfect

The saying is good, there is also a nice
touch to watch, bite your tongue and taste
the sweet blood. Say it and listen carefully.
Listen, take your hand and compare the
old people's long beards, they have turned
grey. Sing a song in a particularly friendly
way, you want to appear funny and maybe
be funny too, so you are somewhere in
between. Since I fell asleep, I haven't had
my say, the thread has broken, the
narrator's tongue is noticeably swollen and
the words come close to me. It may be
rude, but nature doesn't know the excuse.
The grey long old beards flutter in the
wind and give a sublime image, the old
hats with the wide brims are still missing.
Then the day would be perfect.

I promise it

Without looking - I saw you - you gave a
beautiful testimony - the smell of your
worn clothes is in the air - pray briefly and
send wishes to heaven - the optimists
return from the battle - laugh wistfully -
duck - be ashamed - the promise should
be kept - only promised.

Where is the finale

The last thoughts collapse before going to
bed - slip into the next room - and
perceive unfamiliar smells - how does it
work - how does it feel - what becomes of
the body - what becomes of the soul -
where is the final written?

Press

Summarize the day extra briefly,
accidentally crush a fly and feel
uncomfortable. What comes out of the
shallows, you are a squeezer.

Do you accept your thoughts

My secondary thoughts are caught in the
hustle and bustle - the traps are being
reprogrammed - my neighbour was
watching closely - now she is dead and can
go on looking - in retrospect many things
seem sad - there should be determination -
who started it - and why? You do not give
up.

Why not

The day is blue. The evening sweet. The
air is cold. Life laughs. Everything is
getting shorter and shorter. A hunch
emerges out of nowhere. That will also
pass. The inspiration flash quickly
subsided. The room gets darker and the
repetitions remain. Why not.

これが最後のページです

言うことは何も残っていません

私が言えることはすべて
延々と言われてきました

思考は思考をもたらす
最後の考えが魂と共に逃げるまで

その後、すべてが無料で純粋です